Fantasy Monologues for Young Actors

DOUGLAS M. PARKER

A Beat by Beat Book

ISBN-13: 978-0692527566
ISBN-10: 0692527567

For my brother and sister
who chose reality for themselves
and left all the fantasy to me.

TABLE OF CONTENTS

INTRODUCTION

What is a fantasy monologue? All acting, of course, is fantasy to some extent. The situations and characters portrayed in a play or monologue – even if they're based on real events or people – are not, in fact, those events or people. But even so, most plays and monologues are not considered to be fantasy.

Situations and characters that are based on fictional events or people bring us one step closer to fantasy, but even so, most fiction-based plays and monologues have still not achieved the right to be called fantasy.

Quite simply, fantasy requires a "fantastic" situation or character – one that does not exist in the real world. In this book, you'll find monologues for vampires, time travelers, talking animals, characters with unusual powers, kids who live on Mars, and people who simply live in or imagine fantasy worlds of their own creation. Their monologues are Fantasy Monologues because the entire premise is based on fantasy.

WHO IS THIS BOOK FOR?

For the most part, the monologues in this book were created for actors and acting students aged 7-14, as well as for the teachers, directors and acting coaches who work with them. As you look over the possibilities, you'll notice that some of the selections may work better for actors toward the lower end of that age range, while others may work better for actors toward the upper end. Simply choose for yourself or your students the pieces that seem to be the best fit and that offer the best learning, acting or audition possibilities. As you look over the book, feel free to explore at random, as the monologues are presented in no particular order.

A QUICK WORD FOR ACTORS

Every monologue was written to work equally well for male and female actors, which means that any monologue in this book could be right for you. Simply choose whichever pieces appeal to you the most, or allow you to explore particular emotions, situations or acting challenges.

Although some minimal stage directions are given above some of the monologues (or in the text of the monologue itself), feel free to follow or ignore any suggestions made. Quite simply, every monologue is here for you to act, interpret or modify in any way that works best for you. If it helps you to change a word, a name or an action, go ahead and do it. The monologues are merely the canvas, you're the artist.

Finally, as you look over the monologues in this book, always keep in mind that, despite the fact that each character lives in a fantasy universe, they are all still us. Their emotions are the same emotions we have here in the real world. Their desires and needs are just as real to them as yours are to you. Your job is to find the "real" inside the fantasy. Once you do that, you will always be able to bring each character and each moment to life.

Monologues

SPELL

(NOTE: Although the monologue calls for a ruler, if you don't have a ruler handy, a pen or pencil will do. Just be sure to change the words in the monologue accordingly.)

If you believe in something enough, that makes it real. I know that for a fact, because I believe it a lot. Palm reading is real. ESP is real. Magic for sure is real.

(Hold up book.)

See this? It's a book of magic spells from forever ago. Like 1990. Maybe even 1980. It says you need a magic wand to make the spells work, but I'm pretty sure that any kind of stick will do it. Because I believe that a lot.

(Hold up ruler.)

See this? I stole this ruler from my brother. It's like fifteen years old and has a lot of power. I think. Probably. OK, now watch. This is a spell for weather.

(Clear your throat. Be sure to use big, "magical" gestures when casting the spell.)

Clouds - gather overhead.
Skies darken.
Sun go dead.
Air, thicken – turn to black.
Winds roar.
Clouds crack.
Foul breezes howl and blow.
Thunder growl.
Tempest grow.
Earth shake and lightening flash.
Trees break and mountains crash.
Whirlwind shatter, scream and spin.
Lightening, thunder, rain – BEGIN!

(Look around and listen for several moments for any sign of a storm.)

Darn it! Darn it! That always happens.

(Look at your "wand," then throw it on the ground.)

I need to get a better ruler.

1

SMART

OK. So think about it. A pill that makes you super smart. Like Einstein Smart. Like totally super-mega genius you-can-do-anything smart. You just take this pill and you're like . . . smart. So I started, like, totally taking chemistry and biology just to invent this. To make the world, you know, a better, way smarter place. But I ran into, uh, I guess like research slash learning curve issues. I mean, like, I can't even understand, like, a single word of what they say in class. Not one word. How ridiculous is that? And then I figured out my mistake. I should've invented the pill first and then started taking the classes. Oh well – live and learn.

SHADOW

(Your character is a vampire who has grown tired of life.)

There are so many things I miss. Almost everything, really. I thought that becoming a – that being a vampire would be . . . incredible. That living forever – well, that if living at all is good, then that living forever must be so much better. But it isn't like that. After a while, all the things you love about life just become things that you've already done. And then it's all just boredom and repetition. One long, dark night. And people die. At first, just one by one. But eventually everyone. Everyone you've ever known dies and there's just you. And the world goes on and it changes and everything becomes unfamiliar – and you're not a part of it and you can't escape it and it just goes on and on until even the sun is just a memory, and no one at all remembers you even existed. Sometimes even *I* have trouble remembering me. And I know that I've become nothing more than a shadow within the shadows.

LOYALTY

You know, people always say, "loyal as a dog," "he's as loyal as a dog," "just as loyal as a dog" – and I'm sick of it. I mean, it's hard enough just being a dog without having this . . . this expectation placed on you on top of that. It's a little unfair. And it's not like every person out there actually deserves loyalty. Not even close. But you don't want to be the one dog that ruins it for everyone else. Then it's all "bad dog" and "my dog doesn't love me" and "how many times do I have to tell you not to chew up my socks." Like you don't have a whole drawer full of them Todd. And then you'd be surprised how many people just take the whole loyalty thing for granted. Like my owner, Todd. You won't believe this. The other day, he just took this tennis ball and threw it into the farthest corner of the yard. I was *watching* him do it and I thought to myself, "I better get that. Later on, he might want that tennis ball and he won't remember where he put it." So I ran all the way across the yard and brought it back. But was Todd grateful? Not even close. He just took the ball and threw it into another corner of the yard. So I went and got it again. Ridiculous. This went on I don't know how many times and then he didn't even say thank you or let me lick out an ice cream bowl or anything. Hey buddy, ever think that loyalty might be a two-way street? But anyway I got him back later.

 (To the unseen Todd.)

Hey Todd! Go find the sock, boy! Go find the sock!

 (To audience.)

He loves that game.

DYLAN

This is Dylan. Dylan is a stuffed bear, but he's not just any stuffed bear. Dylan used to talk a lot – especially after we first moved here and I really missed my old friends. Then he used to tell me everything. Like how lonely he was. And how much he wished we could move back my old town. And how much he missed my old room. But about a year ago, after I started being friends with Morgan, he started talking less. And then when I started playing soccer and hanging out with everyone from the team he started hardly talking at all. Sometimes if I wake up in the middle the night or if something is really bothering me, Dylan will come over and sit next to me and we'll talk like we used to. But every time, we talk a little bit less – and sometimes I just call one of my friends instead. I think one day maybe Dylan will stop talking completely. But I hope he doesn't.

(Turn to Dylan.)

You won't stop, will you? . . . Dylan?

SLASH

(Your character is in the middle of a sword fight.)

(Lunge forward with your sword.)
Have at you! . . . Take that! And that! And that! . . .
(Your opponent's sword barely misses you as you jump out of the way.)
Whoa! That was close. Someone could lose an eye. . . .
(You advance on your opponent, slashing and thrusting your sword.)
Back! Back! Back! THIS is for robbing the crown jewels.
(You jump back as your opponent's sword almost grazes you.)
Yikes! And THIS is for trying to usurp my throne.
(Dodge out of the way as your opponent's sword just misses you.)
Sheesh! And THIS is for being so unimaginative that you're a bad guy who's actually wearing black. Do you have any idea how ridiculous that is?
(Your opponent gains the advantage and starts chasing you around.)
Hey! Hey! Hey!
(You stop, turn, and start to advance on your opponent, slashing and stabbing with every word.)
I. Will. Not. Let. You. Win! ARGHHH!
(You thrust your sword fatally through your opponent.)
Yeah. How do you like that?
(You pull out your sword and notice how disgusting and bloody it is.)
Ewww. What am I supposed to do with this? Oh well.
(You wipe the sword on your clothes and triumphantly slide it into the scabbard that hangs from your belt. Look down at your opponent's lifeless body.)
OK, Jessie, get up. Now it's your turn to win.
(Stride proudly away from the scene of battle.)

UNICORN

What is it about people and unicorns? I mean, I can't go anywhere without someone yelling "Look! There goes a unicorn!" Or, "Oh my gosh – there really are unicorns!" Or, "Catch it! I think they have magic powers!" To begin with – no, I don't have magic powers. I don't even have fingers. If I even wanted to put on a hoodie or pick up a dime, I'd have to ask someone for help. There's nothing very magical about *that*. And no, if you grab my horn, it does not mean you've captured me. It means you've annoyed me. I *hate* that. And if you think the horn's not sharp, think again. Don't make me prove it. So if you see me walking down the street or in a diner or at the local car dealership, please, just smile, say hello, and maybe ask how my mother's arthritis is doing. Then go away. Because I sure as heck did not move to [NAME OF YOUR TOWN] to make *your* fantasies come true.

PARANOIA

Who says being paranoid is a bad thing?

(Suspiciously, to someone in the audience.)

Was it you?

(To someone else in the audience.)

You? Well, I heard *someone* did. First of all, I don't like people talking about me behind my back. Second, I'm not paranoid. You're all the ones who must be paranoid, the way you watch me all the time. And third, even if I *was* paranoid, which I'm not, that doesn't mean it's a bad thing, or that people need to be hiding behind trees and looking through my bedroom window all the time. That's crazy. Totally nuts. And I'm not saying it's everyone – just most of you. And you know who you are. So, yeah, to all of you who talk about me behind my back and say that I'm paranoid, I just want to say that "paranoid" is just another word for, like, survival instinct. As in survival of the fittest. And if you're all afraid that maybe I'm fitter than you, well then maybe you need to work on your own issues. I'm not the problem. So yeah.

(Look quickly to see if anyone's behind you.)

I gotta go . . . And don't follow me. Bye.

(As you walk off, look behind you several times.)

Bye.

(Exit.)

LIVING LARGE

(Your character is a tough mouse. As you speak, be sure to occasionally do some "mousey" things, like twitch your whiskers, rapidly scratch behind your ear, or whatever else you can think of.)

Bein' a mouse ain't so bad. Ya go where youse want. Do what youse want. Eat what youse want. Well – eat what youse want so long as some gazunk dropped what youse want on the floor or left it out on the counter or it's in some kind a bag or cardboard box or paper wrapper that youse can eat right through. Or if some gazunk threw it in the garbage. Sheesh – youse have no idea what good eats people just throws in the garbage. Fresh cheese. Not so fresh cheese. Cheese that's rotten. Other things. It's like the Olive Garden in there – or maybe the Cheese Garden – but free. A course, bein' a mouse, you got your cats. Youse always gotta be watchin' out for the cats. But even the cats, the way they breed 'em nowadays, I could probably beat half of them myself in a fair fight. Yeah, cats . . .

(Look over both shoulders to make sure no cats are around.)

. . . dey ain't nuttin'. Still, youse better look around and know where the closest hole is to run into. Just in case. And then, when the cat goes away, youse just comes out and goes back to livin' large. Yeah. Bein' a mouse – best life there is. That's what I sez. Best life in the world.

FORGET IT

I have a very cool super power. I mean, I can't pick up buildings or see through clothes or fly through outer space or anything. But it's still pretty amazing. Basically, I can do or say anything I want, and then if I do this

(Do some funny, elaborate gesture - like a funny dance move, or three fast, funny faces in a row, or a loud funny noise.)

. . . it completely wipes it from everyone's memory. So I can actually tell the science teacher exactly what I think of him and then . . .

(Make the gesture.)

. . . Poof. It never happened. Or I can get caught cheating at Monopoly and . . .

(Make the gesture.)

. . . Zap. What missing money? Or I can ask some someone out and if they say no . . .

(Make the gesture.)

Zonk. Never happened. And it can be anything I want. Like, watch.

(Lick your forefinger and get it nice and wet.)

I'm going to go around the room and give everyone here a Wet Willie in the ear and then make you all forget it.

(Make the gesture.)

Want to see it again? Of course, sometimes I wish my secret power also worked the other way. That I could make people remember stuff I *didn't* do. Like make my Mom remember I cleaned my room when I didn't clean my room. Or make my English teacher remember I turned in that book report I never wrote. But even so, making people forget stuff is awesome. I probably shouldn't say anything, but the other day I did the most outrageous, unbelievable and disgusting thing imaginable. If anyone found out about it, I would be in definite trouble. You want to hear about it?

(Pause as though you're about to tell a big story, then make the gesture.)

You want to hear it again? . . . Ahh – forget it.

HELLO SUNSHINE [M]

[Version for Male Actors]

(Your character is the ancient Roman god Apollo, at his weekly psychotherapy appointment.)

Doc, I gotta tell you, this depression is really getting to me. It's just that it's been going on for so long now. Like what – maybe seventeen-hundred, eighteen-hundred years? But I got to admit, I still miss the old days, back when everyone still believed in the old gods. Me, Jupiter, Neptune, Mercury – all the old gang. I mean, for Pete's sake, I'm Apollo the sun god. Every morning, when the sun comes up, that's *me*. I'm still doing *my* job and nobody seems to care. How about somebody sacrificing a goat and saying, "Here's to you, sunshine?" I don't even know when was the last time someone prayed to me. One little prayer – is that so much to ask? All my temples are in ruins. And don't even get me started on the whole animal sacrifice thing. Nothing. Bupkiss. Seriously – it could be a chicken. Someone could sacrifice a raccoon for all I care. How about a cockroach? Just to show that somebody remembers. Just to say, "Hey, thanks for the sunlight." Would that be so much? But no, almost two thousand years and nothing. When they were naming planets, I didn't even get a planet named after me. Even the *sun* isn't named after me. Now that's depressing. And Doc, those pills you gave me last week? For all they do, they could be breath mints. I feel worse right now than when you prescribed them. And I'll tell you something else . . .

(Your unseen doctor interrupts you.)

What? . . . The hour's up already? You've gotta be kidding me.

(The unseen doctor says something else.)

I don't care if Mrs. Kravitz is waiting . . . You know what? Fine. I'll just go sit in a dark room by myself.

(Stand up.)

As if anyone would care. Same time next week?

(Start to exit.)

Fine. See you then.

(Exit.)

HELLO SUNSHINE [F]

[Version for Female Actors]

(Your character is the ancient Roman goddess Aurora, at her weekly psychotherapy appointment.)

Doc, I gotta tell you, this depression is really getting to me. It's just that it's been going on for so long now. Like what – maybe seventeen-hundred, eighteen-hundred years? But I got to admit, I still miss the old days, back when everyone still believed in the old gods. Me, Venus, Jupiter, Neptune – all the old gang. I mean, for Pete's sake, I'm Aurora, the goddess of the dawn. Every morning, when the sun comes up, that's *me*. I'm still doing *my* job and nobody seems to care. How about somebody sacrificing a goat and saying, "Here's to you, sunshine?" I don't even know when was the last time someone prayed to me. One little prayer – is that so much to ask? All my temples are in ruins. And don't even get me started on the whole animal sacrifice thing. Nothing. Bupkiss. Seriously – it could be a chicken. Someone could sacrifice a raccoon for all I care. How about a cockroach? Just to show that somebody remembers. Just to say, "Hey, thanks for the sunlight." Would that be so much? But no, almost two thousand years and nothing. When they were naming planets, I didn't even get a planet named after me. Even the *sun* isn't named after me. Now that's depressing. And Doc, those pills you gave me last week? For all they do, they could be breath mints. I feel worse right now than when you prescribed them. And I'll tell you something else . . .
(Your unseen doctor interrupts you.)
What? . . . The hour's up already? You've gotta be kidding me.
(The unseen doctor says something else.)
I don't care if Mrs. Kravitz is waiting . . . You know what? Fine. I'll just go sit in a dark room by myself.
(Stand up.)
As if anyone would care. Same time next week?
(Start to exit.)
Fine. See you then.
(Exit.)

NICE WORK

You know the hardest thing about being a baby? Nothing. All I have to do is lie here. It's probably the easiest job in the world. Hold on.

(Hiccup, then speak the next line to your mother, who is there, but unseen.)
Me! I am!

(Now speak to the audience again.)
My Mom just asked me who's the cutest little baby in the world, and I know for a fact that it's me. Everybody says so. It's pretty incredible – anything I do, everyone goes crazy. If I hiccup, they tell me how cute I am. If I roll over, they tell me I'm the best little snookie-wookums ever. And if I poop in my pants, you'd think I just wrote the world's best-selling novel. So I do that a lot. I mean, I'm not gonna lie. I love the attention. Hold on.

(Hiccup, then speak the next line to your unseen mother.)
Me! Me! I am!

(Now speak to the audience again.)
Of course, being this awesome can get a little tiring.

(Yawn.)
Even a lot tiring – so I think I'm gonna take a nap now. But don't go away. Everyone says that when I'm sleeping, I look just like an angel.

(Your eyes start to close.)
They say they could watch me for hours.

(Your eyes close. You're almost asleep. You give a tiny hiccup, then speak quietly.)
I am. I am.

(Smile faintly and fall asleep.)

BUS

I write a lot of short stories. I mean a *lot*. And people always get mad at me because the stories always end the same way: The boy gets hit by a bus. I mean, it's always a different boy. And probably a different bus. But that's always the end. And people constantly say to me, "Why did you do that? The boy was right in the middle of all these things and now I'll never know how it ends." But yeah – you *do* know how it ends. *That's* how it ends. And seriously, isn't that the way it *always* ends? Isn't everybody always in the middle of all these things, and then – you know – the bus comes? If you want to read some fantasy where everybody finishes everything they're doing and then lives happily ever after while not doing anything, read Harry Potter. But if you want to read about real life, then go read one of my stories. 'Cuz even though you never know when the bus is going to arrive, you should definitely know it's on its way. And all that stuff you're worried you might be in the middle of? Just finish it. And then do more stuff and finish that too. And then start even more stuff. 'Cuz the story's never actually about the bus. It's about all the stuff you do before the bus shows up.

DINOSAURS

Six weeks isn't a long time. Not when you're [YOUR AGE] and that's all you have. By the time they saw the asteroid coming, that's all we had left . . . I've been thinking a lot about the dinosaurs. The way an asteroid got them too and they didn't even see it coming. Only the very smallest animals survived and a hundred million years later they turned into us and we dug up the dinosaur bones and wondered who they were and what they were like and how they lived. One day maybe the smallest animals here, maybe the mice or the squirrels or the chipmunks, will grow up and they'll rule the earth. They'll dig up our bones and they'll wonder who we were and what we were like and how we lived. But they'll never really know us. Never really know me . . . Or understand why I can't stop thinking about the dinosaurs.

SPIRIT

(Your character is holding séance and you are the medium. A woman is trying to contact the spirit of her deceased husband.)

Now, Mrs. Jackson, give me your hands.

(Hold out your hands for the unseen Mrs. Jackson to hold. Continue to hold her hands for the remainder of the monologue.)

In order for us to contact the spirit of your late husband, I'll need you to close your eyes and place in your mind an image of the deceased. Are you ready?

(Close your eyes.)

Oh spirits on the other side, can you hear us? We who have not yet passed over wish to speak with you . . . Can you hear us? . . . Can you hear us?

(Pause a moment, then open your eyes and speak to Mrs. Jackson.)

I think I got someone.

(Close your eyes and speak to the spirits.)

Oh spirit, we wish to communicate with one who has joined you on the other side. We wish to speak with the spirit of Moe Jackson . . . Thank you, spirit.

(Open your eyes and speak to Mrs. Jackson.)

She's getting him . . .

(Close your eyes again.)

I sense his presence . . . Oh, dweller on the far side, is this the spirit of Moe Jackson?

(Open your eyes.)

It's him.

(Close your eyes.)

Oh spirit from beyond the grave, I am here with your wife and

(The spirit interrupts you.)

. . . What? . . . He's saying . . . He's saying . . . He was just in the middle of watching TV. Do you really need to talk right now? . . .

(Open your eyes as Mrs. Jackson speaks to you.)

What? . . . OK.

(Close your eyes.)

Oh spirit, your devoted wife has asked me to tell you that you have all of eternity to watch TV and would talking to her for two seconds kill you? . . . Ohh . . . Oh I sense his presence very powerfully . . . He says . . . Again with the nagging. How far does a guy have to go to find a little peace? . . . He says, can it wait at least until a commercial?

(Open your eyes as Mrs. Jackson speaks to you.)

What? . . . OK.

(Close your eyes.)

Oh traveler through the spirit world, your wife says . . .

(The spirit interrupts you.)

. . . What? . . . What! . . . No I won't repeat that! . . . No! . . . Well, same to you . . . Hello? Hello?

(Open your eyes.)

I'm afraid we've lost the connection. We'll have to try again some other time, but all things considered, I think that went pretty well.

(Let go of Mrs. Jackson's hands and hold out one hand, palm up.)

That'll be twenty-five dollars.

OPPOSITE

Most people don't know this – and I never really like to talk about it – but I was born on another planet. When I was still a baby, my father put me in this tiny rocket ship that took me to earth, where the atmosphere and the yellow sun and the different gravity all made me different from everyone else. Now, I know what you're thinking: That's just the Superman story. But, first of all, the Superman story is totally made up, and second of all, my story has nothing to do with that. It's actually kind of the opposite. So for instance, the gravity here must be stronger than where I come from, because in gym class everyone makes fun of me because they can all lift bigger weights and run faster and jump higher than me. And the atmosphere here must be thinner, because if I run even a little, I have to breathe really heavy and I get really tired. And the yellow sun here is the worst. Instead of making me not feel any pain at all like Superman, it makes me feel everything. Everyone's mean to me and I feel it all the time. And everyone can tell I'm different and it never stops. I wish I could just go back to where I came from. Where everyone is like me and they're all nice and nothing hurts. But I think that place is gone. And that's why my dad sent me here. So now my real home – the one place where I could be really happy – is just like a memory, or a dream or . . . something. And no matter what I do, I guess this is my life now.

PAIL OF WATER

(Your character is either Jack or Jill from the well-known nursery rhyme.)

You make one mistake and people never forget it. Seriously. I mean, yeah, Jack [or Jill] and me went up the hill to fetch a pail of water. And, yes, one of us fell down and broke his crown and yeah, yeah, the other one came tumbling after. And no – we did not bring back any water. We did not succeed in our mission. And, if I was to be totally honest, we also lost the bucket. But come on. It wasn't like we went up the hill to save the planet from an alien invasion. There wasn't a baby up there about to be eaten by a bear. It was *water*. We fell down. We didn't come back with a pail of water. Someone else got up out of their chair, got a bucket, climbed up the hill and fetched a pail of water. Big deal. Life will go on. And just to set the record straight, I am perfectly capable of fetching water. I personally have fetched hundreds of pails of water, both before that incident and after. So has Jack [or Jill]. It was *one time*. Sheesh. Maybe it's time we all moved on.

WAR

No one knows how it started, or even when. All that's known is that, for as long as anyone can remember, the forks have been at war with the knives. It may have been something as small as whether the fork or the knife should be used to cut a piece of asparagus in half. Or it may have been something much larger – like which was really the most important utensil. No one, of course, paid any attention to the spoons.

Soon, the forks and the knives formed a line on opposite sides of the plate, clashing repeatedly in the middle. The spoons, as we know, sided with the knives. But it really didn't matter, since everyone considered them practically useless – at least until dessert. Year after year, there in the middle of the plate, the knives and forks met again and again. Many sharp words were exchanged and pointed remarks were made. Much flesh was torn and blood was spilled, but neither side would relent.

For several centuries in the Middle Ages, a sort of truce was achieved, which forced everyone to eat with their hands. But nothing lasts forever and soon the forks and knives were at war again, angrily joining the field of battle on plates in every village, town and city. And that's where things stand today. No one knows who will win. And frankly, as a spoon, I couldn't care less.

IRRESISTIBLE

(For the entire monologue, while facing the audience, you're actually looking at your own reflection in an unseen plate glass window. The people you're talking to are actually behind you. As you talk to their reflections in that same window, only look over your shoulder and away from your own reflection every so often, and never for more than a moment.)

(Admiring your reflection.)

I know what you're all thinking. People have been coming up to me all day and saying that I'm irresistible. That it's . . . unnatural. Well, you're right.

(Patting your hair, touching your face, and generally preening.)

It's not natural. Not that I've had surgery or anything. Nothing like that. I mean, I thought it was a joke. I was just walking down the street and this old woman came up to me. Seriously, I thought she was going to ask me for a quarter, but what she said was, "Think you're pretty cute, don't you?" So I said, "Yeah." You know, just to be cute. That was when she said, "How would you like to be irresistible?" She said, "How would you like to be so irresistible that no one can look away?" And just to get rid of her, I said, "OK." And she took my face in her hands and she stared into my eyes with this kind of intense creepy old lady look and then she let go and said, "It's done," and walked away.

I mean, I didn't even really think anything about it, except that it was weird and I should maybe go wash my face. But then I started to notice that people were looking at me. Like *really* looking. Like turning their heads and just staring until they couldn't even see me any more. And people started coming up to me and *telling* me that they couldn't stop looking at me. So I started to wonder if I looked different – if that old woman had actually done something to my face.

(Gradually start to sound more and more scared.)

And so I started running, and then running faster – kind of halfway to get away from everyone and halfway to find a mirror or something, until I saw this store with this big glass window and I stopped and stared at my reflection and it was OK. I was OK. I looked and I looked and my face seemed the same, except that when I was finished, no matter how hard I tried, I couldn't stop looking. I couldn't look away for more than a

21

second. And then all of you started coming up behind me and looking at my reflection too. And you keep telling me and telling me that it's not natural for anyone to be this irresistible and I know it. I KNOW IT! I just want to go somewhere and hide. I just want to go away. But I can't stop looking. *I can't stop looking!*

ELECTION

Hello, my name is Dale Snarly and I'm running for mayor here in [NAME OF YOUR TOWN]. Now, my opponent says that no one here should vote for me, just because I'm a werewolf. He says that no werewolf could possibly represent your interests, and also that I might eat your children. Well, if elected, I promise to work for your interests day and night – except of course during full moons. I will work to clean up the streets, lower taxes, and reduce overcrowding in our schools – only occasionally by eating the children. In the second phase, I will build new parks and new playgrounds for whatever children remain. And always I will be a friend to every citizen, rich or poor, werewolf or human, young or old, tough or tender. So please, if you too believe in a better, less crowded future for our town, vote for Dale Snarly – and together we'll make this town a howling success.

(Howl like a werewolf.)

Now, if anyone would like to have a picture of their baby being kissed by the town's next mayor, please meet me in the parking lot, just after sunset. Thank you!

LIFE ON MARS

(For this monologue, the character starts out very enthusiastic about life on Mars. Gradually, however, your character starts to realize that maybe life on Mars isn't all that great. Be sure to show that shift in tone.)

For hundreds of years, people have wondered about life on Mars. Where is it? Who is it? What's it like? Well, I'll tell you: It's awesome!

(Enthusiastically.)

For one thing, from here, with a telescope, you have this amazing view of the Earth. It's like this giant blue marble, just spinning in the middle of space. And if that's not awesome enough, I'll tell you something else. There's also no weather on Mars. Yeah! Every day of the year, it's 72 degrees. Because you can't go outside . . .

(Beginning to realize that maybe life on Mars is not that great.)

. . . since there's not enough oxygen.

(Trying hard to stay enthusiastic.)

But having to stay inside all the time, you get to be really close with all the other kids! Well, with all nine of them.

(Gradually realizing how hard life on Mars really is.)

'Cuz that's all there are. Ten if you count the baby. Sheesh, I wish there were more kids. Or restaurants. Or stores. Or movie theaters. Or anything! . . . But they teach us all to try and stay positive. Really, really positive. Yeah . . . Did I tell you about the amazing view we have of the Earth?

AWARD

(Your character is a film director accepting an Academy Award, which you are holding as you give your acceptance speech.)

[NOTE: This monologue is written for everyone. If you're a boy, simply change the word "actor" (which appears three times in the monologue) to "actress."]

First, I'd like to thank the Academy for honoring me with this incredible award. Because while it's totally amazing to even be nominated in the company of these other extraordinary film directors, it's even more amazing to beat them. So many people said that it couldn't be done. That no one could direct a version of The Little Engine That Could, starring a centaur and the hologram of an actor who's been dead for over 50 years. Well, we showed them wrong! We showed the world that The Little Engine That Could can still speak to a new generation - and so can an actor who's been dead for over 50 years. And we learned so much more. We learned that holograms are people too. And that some of them are very attractive. And that if a director wants to marry a hologram I should be allowed to. Even if the actor that the hologram is based on has been dead for over 50 years. Aside from that, I'd like to thank my cast and crew, my wonderful parents for having me, and of course the world's most beautiful hologram – my new fiancé! Don't worry honey, we'll get the laws changed! Thank you everyone!

ETERNITY

Love and Eternity. A poem by Alex Brenner.

Out of all of time and all of space,
It was you I fell in love with.

Cavemen discovered fire over thirty thousand years ago,
The Egyptians built the pyramids,
Genghis Khan took over Asia,
Ben Franklin flew a kite.

But out of all of time and all of space,
I happened to grow up in [NAME OF YOUR TOWN],
And go to the same school as you.

We happened to eat lunch at the same table last month,
And you happened to laugh when I choked on my milk.

Maybe in some parallel universe,
There is no you,
Or there is no me,
Maybe [NAME OF YOUR TOWN] doesn't exist,
Or milk hasn't been invented yet,
But that day, in this universe,
Out of all of time and all of space,
All those things came together,
And I fell in love with you.

A lot of people might call that fate,
But honestly, it was just bad luck.

Thank you.

MOMS

Leprechaun moms are the worst. Worse than troll moms, worse than gremlin moms, elf moms, cyclops moms, even succubus moms. I should know, I have one. Yeah, I'm half leprechaun – want to make something of it? So like for instance, the other day I accidentally pushed my little sister by accident. Because accidents happen and that's what that was. And my mom went ballistic. *Now you're grounded. Now you have to apologize. Now you can't watch any TV. Now for talking back to me you're grounded for twice as long* and blah blah blah. And all because of an accident that could've happened to anyone. It was ridiculous. Like not even a centaur mom would be that insane.

So OK, there I was grounded, and about two days later, when I'm supposed to come home directly from school, the battery dies on my cell phone, so I have no idea what time it is and because of that I was maybe all of two hours late for coming home. Two hours tops – it was probably even less. I mean it could've happened to anyone. And my crazy leprechaun mom, she just totally explodes. *Now you're grounded for a month. Now you have to go to bed at 8:30 every night. Now for talking back to me you're grounded for twice as long* and blah blah blah. It was wild. Beyond the bounds of logic. No other mom in the universe would do that. Not even a human mom. Seriously, I think I need a different mom – however you do that. Leprechaun moms are the worst.

RIGHT FIELD

(Your character is in the middle of a baseball game. You're in the outfield.)

(Yelling.)

You got it Brett! You got it! No batter, no batter, no batter!

(To self.)

Sheesh. Baseball has got to be the most boring sport in the world. Shouldn't a sport at least include some exercise? Or moving? Baseball, mostly all you do is stand around. And even when you do run, it's only like 60 feet.

(Yelling.)

What are you, blind ref? That was a strike!

(To self.)

I am so bored. That cloud looks kind of like a giraffe. Or maybe a spoon. Maybe that's why hardly any other countries play baseball, 'cuz it's so boring.

(Yelling.)

Strike him out, Brett! Strike him out!

(To self.)

I bet if aliens came and took over the Earth, they definitely would not start playing baseball. Maybe Foosball. That would be easy to play on a space ship. If they had gravity.

(Yelling.)

Come on! You can do it, Brett! One more strike!

(To self.)

Huh - that cloud is starting to look more like an elephant. Or maybe a ping pong paddle with a really weird handle. I wonder who ever came up with a name like ping pong. Whoever it was . . .

(Yelling.)

Yeah! Yeah! Three strikes! You are *out*, my friend! You are OUT!

(To self.)

Finally. One inning down, eight more to go.

(Start walking offstage.)

Time to go sit around in the dugout for a while.

(Notice the cloud again.)

Huh – now it kind of looks more like a hammer. Whatever.

BLOOM

(Your character is a flower, waiting underground for spring to arrive.)

(Crouch down on the ground, with your hands covering your head.)
Shhhh . . . Can you feel it?
(Uncover your eyes and look left and right.)
Spring is coming.
(Uncover your head slightly and look around a little more. Sniff the air, then look up.)
It's almost here. Every day, the earth over my head gets a little warmer. The days get a little longer. And I get to stretch out a little more.
(Uncover your head completely and look around you.)
I put out one root here.
(Extend a finger on one hand.)
Another root here.
(Extend a finger on the other hand.)
Mmmm – stretching and flexing.
(Uncrouch, just a little bit and extend your hands a little.)
Turning winter into one long, dark memory.
(Uncrouch a little more and extend your hands farther.)
Growing taller. Stronger. Longer. Happier.
(Uncrouch even more and start to stand up.)
Until one day –
(Suddenly stand up, with your arms extended up and out.)
BOOM! Hello, springtime! Ahhhhh.

WIN

It started out as a video game just like any other video game. You shoot a few bad guys, blow up a few buildings, get a few extra lives. You win, you lose, you start over again. But then the food started running out. And when things got really bad, the government figured – why not make the game real? Real winning. Real losing. Real lives. The only thing that isn't real is the game itself. It's still played on a screen, using a laserbox. Just like always. But now – you rescue the princess from the tower? You get to eat that day. You don't rescue the princess? You go hungry. Someone from the other team shoots you? You lose one life. You lose too many lives? Well, you don't have to worry about eating anymore. But the thing is, in the real world, there's less food every day. And everyone can't win. So over time, you start losing more and more of your lives. Until one day, you just have one left. Just one life. And so you sit there, with your hands on the laserbox, just staring at the screen. Waiting. Never looking away. And the princess is waving. She's waving from the tower. And she needs to be rescued. She really, really needs to be rescued. And I'm just so hungry . . . I'm just so hungry.

FREEDOM

(Your character is a boastful pigeon. Begin by strutting around for several moments, bobbing your head, making pigeon noises, turning your arms into wings tucked by your sides and generally acting like a pigeon.)

(Proudly.)

Oh yeah. Take a good look. Pigeon – the last free animal in the world. Not your dog or cat or parrot that's been turned into a . . . gah, I can hardly bring myself to say it . . . into a *house pet*. Not your squirrel that lives off handouts in the park. Not your elephant or giraffe that spend their whole lives in the zoo. Not even your American eagle who practically runs crying from anywhere that people move into. But pigeons? Freedom-loving, free-living pigeons like me? I go where I want, I do what I want, I take what I want. That's right. You want to give me bread crumbs? I will take those bread crumbs. You don't want to give me bread crumbs? I will wait by your feet while you eat your sandwich and then take those bread crumbs anyway.

(Yells.)

FREEDOM!

(No longer yelling.)

You want to move into my neighborhood? *My neighborhood?!?!* I will mess up your statues, your cars and your sidewalks - and then eat your bread crumbs anyway. *Plus* I can fly. Your dog can't do that. And neither can you. Total freedom. Dominion over the earth and sky! Yeah, pigeons! Take my word for it, the beak shall inherit the earth. And if you don't believe me, just wait. Maybe tomorrow, maybe next week, maybe next year, you'll be walking under a tree branch or sitting on a park bench and BOOM! You won't even know what hit you. Well, until you look at your shoulder. Then, obviously, you'll know what hit you. Yeah. A little freedom. And that's a promise you can take all the way to the dry cleaners.

FLYING

There's a scene in Peter Pan where Peter teaches the kids to fly. And the way he does it is, he tells them to think their happiest thoughts. And they do it, and they just start flying. I mean, it tells you right in the book how to do it! So I thought – if they can fly, I bet I can too. So I just started thinking about all the things that made me the happiest. Like the day we picked up my new dog, Rex, from the kennel. And the day I beat my dad at chess – which is also known in my house as the day my dad let me beat him at chess. Or the time my sister gave me a birthday present, when it wasn't even my birthday. Or when my mom says she loves me. And by the time I was finished, even though I was still lying in my bed, I was flying so high I thought I'd never touch the ground again. And I could look down and see everyone and everything in my life and they were all looking up and smiling and waving back at me . . . I don't know if there really is a Peter Pan or an island filled with lost boys and pirates and Indians, but it doesn't matter. Because I know one thing for sure . . . I know how to fly.

JUST RIGHT

Too hard, too soft, too hot, too cold – nothing was ever good enough for her. Not even her name. When she first passed by the house, you think her name was Goldilocks? It was Florence. But like everything else in her life, Florence wasn't good enough for her. Just between us, her hair wasn't even gold. Yeah – that's a dye job. Her hair was a plain mousey brown before a box of Clairol got to it. But I guess "Brownielocks" wasn't good enough for little Miss Complains-A-Lot. And speaking of complaining, what kind of person breaks into other people's houses and then whines about the temperature of the porridge or the softness of the furniture? No – not even other *people's* houses. What kind of person breaks into *a bear's* house and then raises a stink because everything isn't just exactly the way she likes it? Not someone with manners. Not even someone with good sense. Because you know what happens when a person breaks into a bear's house and causes a scene? Let's just say that while Mama Bear, Papa Bear and me didn't think Goldilocks was too sweet, we also didn't think she was too salty. In fact . . .

(Pick your teeth.)

. . . we thought she was just right.

BOOK REPORT [M]

[Version for Male Actors]

(Your character is giving a book report in front of the class.)

My book report is on The Tiran of Labnos – a book that won't be written for another hundred years. And on another planet. I'm well aware, everyone, that you don't believe that I can see into the future and, to be honest, I find it really annoying. And to be honest, I don't find it any consolation whatsoever knowing that in the future you will all *come* to believe it.

Anyhow, in the book, The Tiran of Labnos, which is the subject of my book report, it is discovered that a boy who seems to be an ordinary boy – but who is actually extremely extraordinary – is discovered to be able to see into the future. The main character, to be honest, is based on me. Aliens from the planet of Labnos offer to make this boy the king of the Earth, but, to be honest, the boy is so amazing that he decides to forgive his entire [WHATEVER GRADE YOU ARE IN] grade class, plus everyone else on Earth, for all the ways they've misjudged him and, to be honest, disappointed him. And instead he agrees to be the Tiran of Labnos, which is basically the king anyway, but of a totally different planet. Although this book won't be written for another hundred years, I already know that I'm going to get an A+ on this book report, because . . . you know, the whole seeing into the future thing. The Tiran of Labnos. Thank you.

BOOK REPORT [F]

(Your character is giving a book report in front of the class.)

My book report is on The Tiran of Labnos – a book that won't be written for another hundred years. And on another planet. I'm well aware, everyone, that you don't believe that I can see into the future and, to be honest, I find it really annoying. And to be honest, I don't find it any consolation whatsoever knowing that in the future you will all *come* to believe it.

Anyhow, in the book, The Tiran of Labnos, which is the subject of my book report, it is discovered that a girl who seems to be an ordinary girl – but who is actually extremely extraordinary – is discovered to be able to see into the future. The main character, to be honest, is based on me. Aliens from the planet of Labnos offer to make this girl the queen of the Earth, but, to be honest, the girl is so amazing that she decides to forgive her entire [WHATEVER GRADE YOU ARE IN] grade class, plus everyone else on Earth, for all the ways they've misjudged her and, to be honest, disappointed her. And instead she agrees to be the Tiran of Labnos, which is basically the queen anyway, but of a totally different planet. Although this book won't be written for another hundred years, I already know that I'm going to get an A+ on this book report, because . . . you know, the whole seeing into the future thing. The Tiran of Labnos. Thank you.

ONE DAY

The less there is of something, the more precious it is. Olive trees can live for two thousand years. Giant tortoises for a hundred and fifty. And us mayflies? Twenty-four hours. How amazing is that? A whole life in a single day. You're born at five in the morning, just as the sun starts to color the sky. You get *one* sunrise, but it's a moment that lasts almost forever, casting a golden light across your entire childhood. You leave home at six a.m., then spend hours just exploring the world. And you can fly! Think of it – unlimited freedom in a world where every moment is a day and every perfect minute lasts a month. Years of morning light and summer breezes in a single hour. By eight or nine, you've made friendships that will last a lifetime. A passing cloud changes the face of the world. And always, there's more to see, more to do, more to live as you fly high above the water. By three you've fallen in love, and by four you have a family. Soon the sun, which has been with you always, begins to set. That soft, half-forgotten golden light of your childhood returns. Your own children fly away and newer, smaller suns appear as the night surrounds you. And always, so much left to see. So much left to do. For the first time in your life, the air goes still. The moon rises and explodes with a cool, white light. And still, so many hours – so much life – is left. Who knows what strange, new things could happen next? With so much time. So much life. So many possibilities. All in a single day.

UNITE

(Your character is one of Santa's elves. You're standing in front of an audience of other elves, about to give a speech.)

Is he gone? Is Santa gone? Someone go stand by the door. Cough twice if you see him coming.

(Wait until one of the unseen elves is standing by a door behind your audience.)

OK? Alright.

(Begin your speech to the assembled elves.)

Elves of the North Pole! Throw off your chains!

(Someone interrupts you.)

What? . . . Yes Tim, I know we don't actually wear chains. It's a metaphor. Can I go on now? Thank you.

(Shift back into louder "public speech" mode.)

Throw off your chains! Too long have we slaved without wages.

(You are interrupted again.)

What? . . . Yes Tim, I know there's no place to spend money at the North Pole . . . Yes . . . Yes, I know that everything is free here. That doesn't mean . . .

(Shifting back into "speech" mode.)

That doesn't mean that we elves should be cheated of a decent, living wage! We need payment, not popcorn! Cash, not candy canes! . . .

(Wearily.)

What? Yes Tim, I'm aware of the free massages . . .

(Back in "speech mode.")

But where is the respect! Where are the rewards! Where is it written that elves should be treated worse than the very reindeer who transport the goods we make, yet who work only one day a year! . . .

(Annoyed.)

Yes Tim, of course I know that we only work two hours a day. It's still *work*. Now, can I please just say three words in a row without being interrupted? Thank you.

(Back in "speech mode.")

Workers of the North Pole, unite! We must rise up and seize the means of production! We must . . .

(Pause a moment as you hear something.)

Wait. Was that the lunch bell? It's pizza day today, isn't it? Workers, we'll continue this later, after I've finished my lunch . . . and my after-lunch massage . . . and maybe a nap. Santa won't get away with this much longer! Now let's get in there before all the pepperoni's gone. Thank you.

WRITE & WRONG

(Your character is a pencil that is in the middle of being used to take a test. For the first few lines of the monologue, stand straight and stiff. After that, relax and move more naturally.)

I can't believe this kid is making me write this. Seriously? The capital of Massachusetts is Rhode Island? *Rhode Island?!?!*

(Glance up at the person who is using you to write with.)

Helloooo. It's not too late to fix that. There's a reason I've got an eraser on the top here. I'm not just for writing. I can also be used to correct the lame thing you just wrote. Oh no. Oh no. You did not just use me to write that the District of Columbia – the nation's capital – was named after a country in South America. Sheesh. Why don't you just write that your favorite month of the year is Tuesday? Or that the most common element in the universe is shampoo? How did I wind up with you? I'm serious. They passed around an entire box of pencils. One hundred pencils. And you had to pick me? Sorry. I know I shouldn't be asking you questions. Answers don't seem to be your thing. Still, do you have any idea how embarrassing it's going to be when I'm back in that box with the other pencils, trying to explain how you and I, together, got the lowest grade in the class? I will never get over it . . . Wait a minute . . . What's going on? . . . The kid is putting me down . . . He's raising his hand . . . He's pretending to be sick! YES! He's being excused! He doesn't have to finish the test! The kid pulls through! Phew – that was a close one. I guess in the end, the real lesson here is that life is a test – and the kid and me, we aced it.

CRUNCH

The universe is breathing. In – it gets bigger. Out – it gets smaller. The Big Bang. Then the Big Crunch. Everything comes apart. Then everything comes together. Smaller and denser. Closer and tighter. All drawn together into a black hole. A pinprick at the center of the universe. A tear in the fabric of existence, no bigger than the heart of an atom. But with a gravitational field so dense that nothing can resist it. Not light, not matter, not energy, not thought. The entire universe crashing in on itself. All time and space compressed into a single period at the end of a sentence. Solar systems crushed into a speck of matter. A million galaxies pressed so small they could fit into the palm of your hand and you couldn't even see them. Everything that was once apart, together again, as it was at the beginning. And after all that time. After what seems like an eternity, but can actually be measured in minutes and hours and years – after all that time I'll get to be with you again. I miss you mom.

DRAGONS

I was begging my mom forever.

Can we get a dragon?

No.

Can we get a dragon?

No.

Can we get a dragon?

No.

Finally she broke down and said yes. But when I got to the pet store, the guy had these two really cute dragon pups together in the same cage. He said they were brothers from the same litter and he would only sell them together. When I brought them home, my mom was angry. Crazy angry.

Can I keep them?

No.

Can I keep them?

No.

Can I keep them?

No.

Until finally she broke down and said,

Okay, but these are your *dragons. You* feed them. *You* clean up after them. *You put out any fires they start. And they live in the tool shed in the backyard.*

So fine. Everything is great for about a year and then one day I came home from school and I opened the tool shed and instead of two pairs of glowing red eyes, there was a whole shedful of them. My two dragons totally were not brothers. And now I have like six more baby dragons and my mom will go insane if she knows I have eight dragons in the toolshed. And I don't know what to do. My friend Tim said he might take one, but that still leaves seven. So maybe I'll just try to keep them quiet, pray they don't burn down the tool shed, and hope for the best. As in no more baby dragons. I mean, if I can just keep the two big ones apart, maybe the little ones are all brothers, right?

THOUGHTS

Now I know what you're thinking. Seriously, I actually know what you're thinking.

(Directly to various audience members.)

No.

Yes.

Same to you.

I'll tell you later.

(To the general audience.)

For as far back as I can remember, I've been able to . . . not exactly hear people's thoughts, but *know* what they're thinking. Whenever I'm with people – whether I want to or not – it's just there. Always. It's like being in a crowd and everyone's talking at me at once – even if no one's talking. Even when I'm alone with someone, there's always so much coming at me. What they're saying and what they're thinking. The lie at the same moment as the truth. People asking what *I* want to do when I already know the only thing *they* want to do. Always there – unless I'm alone. Always two voices, or ten, or a hundred. All coming at me.

(Gradually getting louder.)

Fighting with each other and crowding out everything else. Filling my head until there's no space left for me to think my own thoughts. And it has to stop! IT HAS TO STOP!

(Quietly.)

All I want is a little quiet. All I want is to be alone. Because I can't start thinking . . . until you stop.

POTION [M]

[Version for Male Actors]

OK, OK, OK. So I have to admit it. I've had this humongous crush on this girl Morgan for maybe forever. She sits right in front of me in math, and also one desk up and three desks to the right in Social Studies, plus two desks back and three desks left in American History. But the thing is, she's never liked me at all. Not even a little. So last week I developed this awesome plan where I would create this love potion and then get Morgan to drink it and then, you know, she'd totally like me too. Radically foolproof. The only thing is that I don't actually know anything about how to make a love potion. So what I did was, I just put in pretty much anything I could think of because, obviously, if I put in enough things, some of them would have to be the right ones, right? So I put in salt and sugar and almost everything else in my mom's spice rack, plus aspirin, rubber bands, motor oil, grass clippings, a bunch of different flowers, a pine cone, laundry detergent, a dead bee, some chicken bones and, I don't know, a bunch of other stuff. Then I let it sit for three days, put it in a Pepsi can and asked Morgan if she wanted a sip. And she drank it! It was perfect. But here's the thing. I think one or maybe even two of the ingredients must have been wrong. Because after she finished throwing up, instead of telling me she loved me, she told me that she hated me. Failure on a massive scale! But it's actually OK. After seeing her throw up, I'm kind of over her now anyway.

POTION [F]

[Version for Female Actors]

OK, OK, OK. So I have to admit it. I've had this humongous crush on this boy Morgan for maybe forever. He sits right in front of me in math, and also one desk up and three desks to the right in Social Studies, plus two desks back and three desks left in American History. But the thing is, he's never liked me at all. Not even a little. So last week I developed this awesome plan where I would create this love potion and then get Morgan to drink it and then, you know, he'd totally like me too. Radically foolproof. The only thing is that I don't actually know anything about how to make a love potion. So what I did was, I just put in pretty much anything I could think of because, obviously, if I put in enough things, some of them would have to be the right ones, right? So I put in salt and sugar and almost everything else in my mom's spice rack, plus aspirin, rubber bands, motor oil, grass clippings, a bunch of different flowers, a pine cone, laundry detergent, a dead bee, some chicken bones and, I don't know, a bunch of other stuff. Then I let it sit for three days, put it in a Pepsi can and asked Morgan if he wanted a sip. And he drank it! It was perfect. But here's the thing. I think one or maybe even two of the ingredients must have been wrong. Because after he finished throwing up, instead of telling me he loved me, he told me that he hated me. Failure on a massive scale! But it's actually OK. After seeing him throw up, I'm kind of over him now anyway.

FLEE

Used to be a good life round these parts. It's natural ain't it? Flea finds a good spot on a dog, course he's gonna settle in, find a wife, raise a family. It's natural. Why there's a family over by the tail they say that's been here for twelve generations. Couldn't stand it down that way myself. The smell, you know. But to each his own. Me, I live over by a really nice clump of fur under Sparky's left armpit. Yeah, Sparky's the name a the dog we all live on. Leastwise, we lived on him til today. I don't even know how to say it. This morning, a cousin a mine that lives over by the right ear heard Sparky's owner sayin' she was takin' him to the groomer for a flea bath tomorrow. Now we're all scrambling to get out.

Over by the rump, there are whole families what have lived here as long as anyone can remember, holdin' onto their babies and cryin' – lined up all the way down both hind legs, just waiting for a chance to get to the cat. Some of the younger kids are talkin' 'bout goin' wild – maybe findin' somethin' in the walls to live on, like a mouse or even a squirrel, and taking their chances. I even heard some fellas talkin 'bout tryin' to find a nest a robins someone said they once saw in the attic. But that's just desperation. Fleas was never meant to fly. And it ain't like anyone could survive a trip all the way to the attic anyway.

Me – I remember when I was little, seein' a raccoon livin' under the floorboards in the front porch. Sparky walked right over him. If I could just get my family onto that raccoon the next time Sparky's owner lets him out, I think we'd be alright. It's got lots a hair and I think it'd be warm under that porch in the winter and cool in the summer. But nothin's for sure. It's been a long time since I seen that raccoon and sometimes Sparky's owner lets him out the other door anyway. So we just sit here and wait. Me and my family. We just sit here and hope we can make it out before the end. What other choice we got?

EDEN [M]

[Version for Male Actors]

(Your character is Adam, in the Garden of Eden.)

I wonder if Eve really likes me. I mean, I know that she was made out of my rib and everything and that I'm like the only other person in the world and all. But still – what if she's just faking it? OK, OK – she *does* laugh at my jokes and such, but what does that really mean? I mean neither of us has ever actually *heard* a joke before. What if my jokes aren't even funny and she isn't laughing *with* me, she's laughing *at* me. That would be mean. I mean, like if she doesn't even really like me and then she's also laughing *at* me. Oh my gosh, and then she's also laughing about the fact that she's laughing at me and I don't even know that she's doing that. Except that I do know it now. If that's what's happening. Why are girls so complicated? OK, I've had it. I am not going to let someone like Eve laugh at me any more. Even if she *is* the only girl in the world. I am totally breaking up with her. Like right now . . . But then who would tell me how smart I am? And good at hitting rocks with sticks. And funny. Oh right. She actually does say that she thinks I'm funny. So OK. So OK. So OK. I am not breaking up with Eve today. Or probably tomorrow. But the next time I even think she's making fun of me, it's over.
> *(Yell.)*

You hear that, Eve!?!? It will be OVER!
> *(Look around and notice that Eve is nowhere around you. More quietly.)*

. . . Eve? . . . Pookie? . . . Where are you?
> *(Look in the distance.)*

Phew – there she is on that hill.
> *(Yell, to Eve.)*

Hey, Eve? Why don't we have some fruit with dinner! Maybe we can finally try those apples!
> *(To self.)*

Nice.

EDEN [F]

(Your character is Eve, in the Garden of Eden.)

I wonder if Adam really likes me. I mean, I know that ever since I was made out of his rib and everything I'm like the only other person in the world and everything. But still – what if he's just totally faking it? OK, OK – he *does* laugh at my jokes and such, but what does that really mean? I mean neither of us has ever actually *heard* a joke before. What if my jokes aren't even funny and he isn't laughing *with* me, he's laughing *at* me. That would be mean. I mean, like if he doesn't even really like me and then he's also laughing *at* me. Oh my gosh, and then he's also laughing about the fact that he's laughing at me and I don't even know that he's doing that. Except that I do know it now. If that's what's happening. Why are boys so complicated? OK, I've had it. I am not going to let someone like Adam laugh at me any more. Even if he *is* the only guy in the world. I am totally breaking up with him. Like right now . . . But then who would tell me how smart I am? And good at arranging rocks. And funny. Oh right. He actually does say that he thinks I'm funny. So OK. So OK. So OK. I am not breaking up with Adam today. Or probably tomorrow. But the next time I even think he's making fun of me, it's over.

(Yell.)

You hear that, Adam!?!? It will be OVER!

(Look around and notice that Adam is nowhere around you. More quietly.)

. . . Adam? . . . Pookie? . . . Where are you?

(Look in the distance.)

Phew – there he is on that hill.

(Yell, to Adam.)

Hey, Adam? Why don't we have some fruit with dinner! Maybe we can finally try those apples!

(To self.)

Nice.

LANGUAGE

Doctor. Dolittle. Seriously? The movie makes no sense. The guy can talk to *all* the animals? *All* of them? Like "Animal" is a language? That's like someone from Jupiter writing a book where the main guy talks "Human" and can talk to everyone on earth. Hello – no one here talks Human. We talk like American or Chinese or French or whatever. But *no one* talks Human and we definitely don't all talk the same thing. Same thing with animals. It took me like three years of studying, PLUS a private tutor, PLUS a lot of time in the basement just to *start* talking rat.

You're surprised aren't you? Everybody wants to talk dog or maybe cat, but I'm telling you there are a lot more rats than there are dogs or cats. And they know *everything.* Even if you can't see them, rats are everywhere – in your house, your school, the mall, the supermarket, the park – everywhere. And they hear everything. If you've got a secret, it's not a secret from the rats. If you did something that's embarrassing or that you shouldn't have done, I can tell you right now, the rats are all talking about it. And they're talking about it to me. It's awesome. So keep your Doctor Dolittle and your dog talk and your cat talk. If you need me, I'll be down in the basement with my rat dictionary and my rat tutor just practicing and practicing. And if you got a problem with that, just remember, I know all your secrets. And I know exactly how to rat you out.

ADVENTURE

(Your character is giving a report to the class, using a remote control to change the photos that are being projected onto a screen behind you.)

OK, so this summer I took a trip to South America with my mom, my little brother Jackson and my dad. My dad is an anthropologist. That's from the Greek word *anthro* meaning mankind and *pologist* from the Greek word for apologize – I think. So basically, my dad goes all over the world figuring out why mankind does the things it does and then apologizing for it. This trip, we went to South America, to figure out why the remote Indian tribes there do whatever it is that they do.

(Click the remote to project a photo on the screen behind you.)
This is a picture of us getting off the boat.

(Click the remote to change the photo on the screen behind you.)
This is a picture of me and my family with our guide Pablo.

(Click the remote to change the photo.)
This is Pablo getting captured by the Jaguar Tribe, way up in the Amazon rainforest.

(Click the remote.)
This is my mom, dad and Jackson getting captured.

(Click the remote.)
This is a selfie of me hiding behind a tree.

(Click the remote.)
This is a picture of me saving the daughter of the chief of this other tribe called the Monkey People from drowning. It's actually pretty funny because I didn't know that I was saving her from drowning. I actually thought she was just this huge fish, and I was really hungry.

(Click the remote.)
This is a picture of me being made the new chief of the Monkey People.

(Click the remote.)
Now here I am discovering a gold mine.

(Click the remote.)
And this one's a diamond mine.

(Click the remote.)

And this one's a plutonium mine. As it turns out, there are actually a lot of mines in the Amazon rainforest that no one knew about. And they're super easy to find!

(Click the remote.)

This is me using the money I got from the mines to build a bunch of schools and libraries and stuff for the Monkey People.

(Click the remote.)

This is me meeting the president of United States.

(Click the remote.)

And the president of Russia.

(Click the remote.)

President of Brazil.

(Click the remote.)

The pope.

(Click the remote.)

Movie star.

(Click the remote.)

Movie star.

(Click the remote.)

Rock star.

(Click the remote.)

Another president.

(Click the remote.)

Movie star.

(Click the remote.)

Billionaire.

(Click the remote.)

And here I am saving my mom, dad, Jackson and Pablo from their captivity with the Jaguar Tribe. Sorry mom. Sorry dad. Sorry Jackson and Pablo. I didn't know where you were until then.

(Click the remote.)

And here we are getting back on the ship.

(Click the remote.)

And this is the most amazing ice cream buffet ever that they had on the ship. You could totally eat as much as you wanted and then go back for even more.

(Click the remote.)

And here we are getting off the ship.

(Click the remote.)

And here we are in front of my house.

(Click the remote.)

And this is my hamster, Toby. Overall, it was a pretty cool summer and I can't wait to find out what part of mankind we visit next year and apologize for.

BRAINS

(Your character is a zombie.)

The day I got bitten by Fred was probably the best day of my life. Well, technically it was also the last day of my life, since Fred is a zombie – but what a relief. Before I got bit, my dad was all like, "What are you going to do with your life," and "Casey, you need to have a goal – one thing that's important to you." Now, I definitely have a goal. Brains. They're *totally* important to me. Seriously. Like, eating brains is all I think about. And it's even something my dad and me can share. If you know what I mean.

(Lick your teeth.)

Even my little sister Dorothy sometimes comes out with us. Being zombies has definitely brought us together as a family. So yeah, thank you Fred. Before you bit me, I was lost. Didn't know what I wanted to do with my life. But now that my life is over, I finally understand that all it takes to get a head is to grab it and then bite into it. Mmm, brains.

DRIFT

(Your character is drifting at sea in a lifeboat. NOTE: Although the monologue indicates that your companion Kelly is a girl, if you'd prefer Kelly to be a boy, simply change the word "she" (which appears three times in the monologue) to "he.")

Gosh, I wish I had some food. Or some water. Or even a fishhook. They call this a lifeboat, but they don't put any of the things in it that you need to live. There's nothing here. Just the ocean. And the clouds. And the sun . . . And Kelly. I don't think Kelly's going to make it. She looks bad. She doesn't even talk anymore. Just lies there and moans. She's driving me crazy.

(To Kelly.)

Kelly. Kelly – are you OK?

(To self.)

Nothing.

(To Kelly.)

It's going to be OK. Can you hear me? It's going to be alright.

(To self.)

I don't even know if I believe that. But if I could just . . . If I could just make Kelly believe what I'm saying, I might start to believe it, too.

(To Kelly.)

Don't worry, Kel. I'm right here. I'm right here and I promise you I'm not going anywhere.

(To self, after a pause.)

. . . I'm not going anywhere.

ONE WISH

(Your character is a genie.)

The bottle I'm trapped in is made of blue glass. And if you picked it up and stared through the glass, you would see what looks like a tiny blue genie. Just one. Just me. Looking out . . . From inside the bottle, staring out through the glass, the whole world looks blue. I see a blue sun over a blue tree, surrounded by blue clouds. Blue dogs run past me. And blue dust blows by and buries the bottle. But once in a while – not once every few months or every few years, but once every few centuries, someone finds the bottle. Finds me. And if they're smart enough, or if they don't like dirt, or sometimes even just by accident, sometimes someone rubs the bottle. And I get to come out. I get to breathe the air. Feel the wind. And see a yellow sun, floating between white clouds. It's the best, worst moment you can ever imagine. Because I can grant anyone in the universe three wishes, but I can't even grant myself *one*. And all I want is the simplest thing in the world – to just walk away. Leave the bottle. And just be free . . . I don't understand it. Every single person that finds me already has everything I've ever wanted and all they want is . . . more. Not one of them ever bothered to ask if they could set aside one wish and do the smallest, the biggest, the only thing in the world for me. Set me free.

BIOLOGY CLASS

(NOTE: Whatever gender you are, Elrog is the opposite gender. So, although the monologue indicates that Elrog is a boy, if you're a boy yourself, simply change a few words in the second half of the monologue to make Elrog a girl.)

When they first landed, everyone was all like, "Oh my gosh, they're here to take over the Earth." And there was just so much drama. I mean, like, just because they're from another planet doesn't mean they're, like, bad people. Well, I mean, they're not people at all. But you know what I mean. It doesn't mean they're bad. But no one would listen to me. I don't even know how many fights I got into about it with, like, my mom and my dad and my best friend Alex and what*ever*. So boring. But then, after a while, after all the drama died down, people were all just like, whatever, these aliens are actually pretty cool. Like for instance, this one alien in my biology class named Elrog or something like that, he totally tells the funniest knock-knock jokes. I'm not kidding. Like what Earthling can even make *one* knock-knock joke funny and this guy has a ton of them. At least I think it's a guy. Anyway, whatever, he's super cute and I think I'm going to ask him to the school dance. I don't even want to know what my mother will have to say about that. So much drama. Not looking forward to that conversation.

ROOMS

In the dream, I'm always in my own house, in my own room. I get up and walk down the hallway and I see this door that I've never seen before, and behind it is this room that I never knew was there and I'm totally amazed that it could be right in my house and I never knew it. And it's beautiful, with big windows and really high ceilings. And off of it is another room and another room and another room, all right there in my house. I read somewhere online that your dreams are just your subconscious trying to tell you something, and I think what my dream is trying to tell me is that the door, and all these other rooms are just the parts of me that I haven't discovered yet. And that beyond the rooms that I know are other rooms of me, leading to other rooms and then other houses and other towns and other cities and then to whole other worlds of me. And I believe it. Now all I have to do is find the door.

TIME OUT

When my dad first invented the time machine, he couldn't of been more annoying. No one but him was allowed to touch it. He'd go on one of his adventures and then reappear in the living room all like, "Hey, I just saw Christopher Columbus discover America!" Or like, "I just watched a gladiator fight in ancient Rome!" But then one night, my dad came into my room and said, "Want to go hunt some dinosaurs this weekend?" And then he pulled out a bunch of cameras and yelled, "Family photo safari!" Oh. My. Gosh. As soon as we stepped out of the time machine I knew this was going to be good. Everywhere there were, like, stegosauruses to take pictures of and brontosauruses to take pictures of and tyrannosauruses to take pictures of. It was awesome. There were even, like, little tiny dinosaurs that you could feed ferns to and stuff. Anyway, my dad and me spent the entire weekend walking around together and saying, "Look at that! . . . Look at that!! . . . Look at THAT!!!" I wish I could say that there was one really big moment where my dad pulled me out of the jaws of a giant pterodactyl or something. But really, what he did was even more amazing. He pulled the world's most awesome weekend out of thin air. Well, him and the time machine. But I think my dad totally deserves at least half the credit.

I, PHONE

(Your character is selling a new product in a television commercial. Try to overact a little and really "sell" your product.)

Hi everyone. I'm here to tell you about a smart new product called the Smart Chip. It's the totally awesome, next-generation upgrade to your Smart Phone. And it's so easy and convenient that it's actually implanted directed into you.

Before I had my Smart Chip implanted, sometimes someone would ask me a question and I would actually say, "I don't know," or "Let me find out." But now that I have my Smart Chip, I *always* know. Everything. And not just little facts and trivia, but all of literature, art, astronomy, history, psychology, geography, chemistry. *Everything.* It's that easy. And that convenient.

Better still, if I want to talk to someone, all I have to do is just think their name and if they've got a Smart Chip too, it's like I suddenly already know what they were going to say anyway, so why bother? And best of all, if someone without a Smart Chip asks me how I feel about something, the Smart Chip will *tell* me how I feel about it. And what I want to do. And where I want to go. And how to behave in every situation. What a time-saver!

The truth is, now that I have my Smart Chip, I don't even have to think anymore at all. Or read. Or talk to people. Or go outside. Or do *anything*. It's like I've already done it all. Inside my head. Smart Chip is *that* convenient.

To find out if a Smart Chip is right for you, have one implanted today. Smart Chip – the last decision you'll ever need to make.

PARADE [M]

[Version for Male Actors]

Why is that girl looking at me? *Is* she looking at me? I think she's looking at me. I mean, obviously she's looking at me. I'm the prince. Plus I'm sitting on a really tall horse in the middle of a parade. But is she looking at me just because I'm the prince, or because she likes me? It's really hard to tell. People gush all over me all the time – even the ones that *don't* like me. And then there are the ones that *think* they like me, just because I'm a prince, but they don't *really* like me – not for myself. They just like the idea of liking a prince. Of course, maybe I just like the idea of liking her because she's a peasant. Peasants are cool – up to a point. Anyway, I'm already way past her and she didn't even bother to follow my horse, so I guess that answers that question. Wait a second. Who's this? Is she looking at me? She's *definitely* looking at me.

(Sit up straight and look as regal as you can.)
Oh yeah, peasants are cool.

PARADE [F]

Why is that guy looking at me? *Is* he looking at me? I think he's looking at me. I mean, obviously he's looking at me. I'm the princess. Plus I'm sitting on a really tall horse in the middle of a parade. But is he looking at me just because I'm the princess, or because he likes me? It's really hard to tell. People gush all over me all the time – even the ones that *don't* like me. And then there are the ones that *think* they like me, just because I'm a princess, but they don't *really* like me – not for myself. They just like the idea of liking a princess. Of course, maybe I just like the idea of liking him because he's a peasant. Peasants are cool – up to a point. Anyway, I'm already way past him and he didn't even bother to follow my horse, so I guess that answers that question. Wait a second. Who's this? Is he looking at me? He's *definitely* looking at me.

(Sit up straight and look as regal as you can.)

Oh yeah, peasants are cool.

GROUP THERAPY

(Your character is the moderator in a group therapy session for clones. The monologue begins just as the group members – your fellow clones – are arriving.)

Hi everyone, come on in. Now, as you all know, we're here to process our feelings about being clones. Why doesn't everyone start by grabbing a chair?

(Indicate a place to your left.)

Pat, you sit over here.

(Indicate a place in front of you.)

Pat, why don't you sit here?

(Indicate a place to your right.)

And Pat, why don't you come sit over on this side? Well, my name is Pat and I'll be leading the group today. Why don't we begin by talking about our feelings about being clones? As you all know, we were all originally cloned from the same person - Pat McGillicuddy - so we've got a lot in common.

(The group member on the left raises a hand to make a comment.)

Yes, Pat . . . Well, I think I speak for everyone here when I say that we all feel that exact same way.

(The group member on the right makes a comment.)

Yes. Pat? . . . You raise an interesting point. Is there anyone here who *doesn't* agree with what Pat just said? . . . I didn't think so.

(To the group member in front of you who hasn't spoken yet.)

Aaand Pat, you're being awfully quiet. Is it because you're thinking that one thing that we're all thinking, but don't want to say? . . . Yeah. Well, why don't we save that and not talk about it next time? Great. Well, I think we've made a lot of progress today and I look forward to sharing and getting to know each other even better next time. Why don't we all give ourselves a round of applause.

(Gently clap for a moment.)

Now everyone please remember to put your chair back against the wall where you found it and then let's all go back to our regeneration pods and try to get a good night's sleep.

RISE

At first, just as the rocket is lifting off, all you can feel is this crushing weight. Everything feels heavy – your arms, your legs, it's hard to breathe. It's just the weight of your own body, but pinning you down at four times the force of normal gravity as the rocket accelerates up and through the clouds. It's the Earth trying to pull you back. It doesn't want to let you go. But the rocket is stronger. For just those few moments, the rocket is stronger than the world and you rise and rise. Beyond people. Beyond mountains. Beyond clouds. Until the crushing pressure drops away. And the weight. And the world. Until you've broken free and you start to float. Still strapped in your seat, but floating, weightless, and freer than you've ever been. And you turn and look out the window and there it is, floating too – the whole world. Everything you've ever seen or known or experienced, distilled to one pure drop of beauty. And just for a moment, you realize that you're no longer a part of it. That the Earth is one world and you are another. And then it disappears from view.

NOTES

NOTES

ABOUT THE AUTHOR

DOUGLAS M. PARKER is an award-winning playwright and lyricist, as well as the author of the best-selling *Contemporary Monologues for Young Actors*. His theatrical works include the musical, *Life on the Mississippi* (book and lyrics), based on Mark Twain's classic autobiographical coming-of-age tale; *BESSIE: The Life and Music of Bessie Smith*, based on the rise and fall of the great American blues singer; *Thicker Than Water*, a drama based on the Andrea Yates tragedy; *Declarations*, a Young Audience historical drama drawn from the letters of John and Abigail Adams from their earliest courtship through the summer of 1776; and *The Private History of a Campaign That Failed*, a Young Audience comedy based on Mark Twain's true, humorous memoire of his time as a lieutenant in the Confederacy's least accomplished, most forgotten regiment. He can be reached at MonologueFrog@gmail.com.

Printed in Great Britain
by Amazon